The Unparalleled Beauty
of a Crooked Line

ALSO BY GINNY LOWE CONNORS

Barbarians in the Kitchen (poems, 2005)
Under the Porch (poetry chapbook, 2010)

The Unparalleled Beauty
of a Crooked Line

Poems by

Ginny Lowe Connors

Antrim House
Simsbury, Connecticut

Copyright © 2012 by Virginia Lowe Connors

Except for short selections reprinted for purposes of
book review, all reproduction rights are reserved.
Requests for permission to replicate should
be addressed to the publisher.

Library of Congress Control Number: 2012947340

ISBN: 978-1-936482-32-0

Printed & bound by Sheridan Books, Inc.

Book Design by Rennie McQuilkin

Front Cover Artwork by Virginia Dehn

Author Photograph by Brian Ambrose

Antrim House
860.217.0023
AntrimHouse@comcast.net
www.AntrimHouseBooks.com
21 Goodrich Road, Simsbury, CT 06070

For Marty

and for Dan, Cindy, Adam, and Owen

Acknowledgements

Grateful acknowledgment to the editors of the following publications, in which these poems first appeared, some in slightly different forms:

Argestes: "Illusion as Snake in the Grass." *Blueline:* "Untethered." *Broken Bridge Review:* "Zen Garden." *Caduceus:* "Thirteen Ways of Looking at a Classroom." *Connecticut Review:* "Living Room," "You Reappear." *Eclipse:* "Wheat Field with Crows." *Encore: Prize Poems, National Federation of State Poetry Societies:* "Mother in the Month of May / I," "Ordinary Time." *English Journal:* "Trying to Teach Travis." *Everybody Says Hello:* "Great Blue Heron at Elizabeth Park." *Jane's Stories:* "Her Turn in the Desert." *Madison Review:* "Under the Porch." *Perigee:* "Sweet Molasses." *SEEK IT: Writers and Artists Do Sleep* (Red Claw Press): "The Snore." *Spillway:* "Wind and a Black Horse." *Spotlights* (Northwest Cultural Council): "Balloon Man." *Theodate:* "Silence and Disorder." *Tiger's Eye:* "Cold Crow Weather."

In addition, several of the poems in this book are included in a chapbook, *Under the Porch,* published by Hill-Stead Museum in 2010.

"Balloon Man" won the Northwest Cultural Council Contest: Life's Unique Journey. "Her Turn in the Desert" won 4th prize in the *Jane's Stories* Press Contest for Women Writers, 2008. "Mother in the Month of May / I" won the Mothers and Daughters Award, sponsored by the National Federation of State Poetry Societies. "Ordinary Time" won the Winners Circle Award, sponsored by the National Federation of State Poetry Societies. "The Snore" was performed by the East Haddam Stage Company in a production entitled *Plays and Poetry.* "Sweet Molasses" won second prize in the Perigee Poetry Contest, 2009.

Thank you to the artists who inspired some of these poems.

In the poem "A Book, a Bird, a Question," the words "the valise opens and a bird rides out on the wind through a door" are from an essay by Nance Van Winckel entitled "Staking Claim to the Title."

This book would not have come into being without the wise insights offered by Rennie McQuilkin, and without the help and support of the good friends in my writing group, Partners in Poetry: Christine Beck, Sherri Bedingfield, Tere Foley, Pat Hale, Bob Jacob, Nancy Jarasek, Julia Paul, and Elaine Zimmeran. I offer my heartfelt thanks also to Leslie Ullman, Natasha Sajé, Mark Cox, David Wojahn, and Robin Behn, who guided me through revision of some of the poems.

Table of Contents

I. WHY

Mother in the Month of May, I / 5
Wind and a Black Horse / 7
Why / 9

II. COLD CROW WEATHER

Under the Porch / 13
Sweet Molasses / 15
Silence and Disorder / 17
Optical Longings and Illusions / 19
Cold Crow Weather / 20
Locked In / 22
Playing House / 24
Taste of Winter / 27
Mother in the Month of May, II / 29
A Bird, a Book, a Question / 30
Mother in the Month of May, III / 31
Untethered / 32
What Comes to Us / 33
A Field in August / 34
Goodbye, Goodbye / 36
Still Life with Goldfish / 37
Wolf Tracks / 38
A Sea of Stingrays / 39
Her Turn in the Desert / 41
On the Day of Her Death / 43
The Path Through Mystery Is Never a Straight Line / 44
Legacy with Light and Shadow / 46
Wheat Field with Crows / 48
Trying to Teach Travis / 49

Thirteen Ways of Looking at a Classroom / 50
Boys / 54
Living Room / 56
Kandahar / 58
Zen Garden / 59

III. BLUE DOOR

Evolution as Longing and Escape / 63
Ambition / 65
Periscope / 68
The False Mirror / 70
Double Vision / 71
As We Were Leaving the National Zoo / 72
Because of the Oranges / 74
Lunar Eclipse / 76
Illusion as Snake in the Grass / 77
Manatee / 78
In Flight / 80
The Unparalleled Beauty of a Crooked Line / 81
Balloon Man / 82
The Snore / 84
Ordinary Time / 85
You Reappear / 87
Your Heart, Like a Wild Bird, Lands in the Middle of a Life / 88
Red Balloon / 89
Great Blue Heron at Elizabeth Park / 90
Lotus with Seeing Hand / 91

ABOUT THE AUTHOR / 93

ABOUT THE BOOK / 94

The Unparalleled Beauty of a Crooked Line

I. Why

Mother in the Month of May / I

Steam in the kitchen and my mother
leaning into it. Wax wrappers from the butter

and squares of chocolate litter the counter.
The sweet scent of sorrow—my mother

is making fudge. All she knows to do
is to drop small drabs of chocolate

into the glass of water
to see if the fudge will harden.

Little journey in a glass—
we consider it together. Her face

is flushed. She looks like somebody else,
eyes nervous; they won't look my way.

Across the hall I hug my grandfather hard.
He squeezes his eyes closed, slowly

shakes his head. From his old leather chair
he bends down every few minutes

to stroke the fur of his shepherd,
black patience with her chin on her paws.

It's the deceitful month of May.
Trees outside blossom pink and white.

"Mother, may I?" The children's voices float toward us
as they step forward in a game I've left behind.

There is to be no funeral.
Death's just a hole in the fabric.

It's a mystery, what happened—
first my grandma was here and then

she was not. We don't speak of it. No words
have been invented that can describe

this vanishing. But for weeks,
months, a silent snow sifts stubbornly

through my dreams. So begins my life
with white paper, trying to name that silence,

touch with one finger the warm breath
that clouds the glass in all my empty rooms.

Wind and a Black Horse

shifting beneath the wind
white   fields of white

beneath the wind a shifting

like the stories of my grandmother
written in invisible ink   white

on white paper
invisible ink   the wind   the wind

scrawls its message in the snow
and a black horse rears up   the whites
of its eyes showing

its eyes showing   the horse
rearing up in the story my grandmother heard

and her small brother   leaning against her
heard it too   fell into the story

not tearing up
"I'm not crying   I just have a cold in my eyes"

shifting far beyond me her own eyes
as she tells me this

as I tell it now to you   but I am cold

close the windows—cold   shut the door
wind shuffles the pages   the facts

no such thing as a fact—
if there is
sometimes the wrong ones
make the stories right

wronged   the stoutest hearts
keep pounding do you hear hooves

a wind shifts through us
          something rears up

through drifts of snow   again
again   I watch a black horse gallop

Why

Because the page listens without talking back.
Because I'm lost in a forest and out of white stones.
Because a voice in a dream demanded this of me.
Because I'm obedient.
Because I'm rebellious.
Because I can do nothing else.
Because the page is my wilderness and each letter a sign.
Because words weave spells that protect me from evil.
Because words knock against me until I hurl them into a poem.
Because I can fold a poem up and hide it under my mattress.
Because I'm a fool.
Because I'm a genius.
Because I want to.
Because I watched someone's memory sail off to a distant country.
Because it's raining and the old snow is melting.
Because I'm sad.
Because I'm in love.
Because I can.
Because tomorrow the wind may blow me away.
Because a black horse in white snow told me to write this down.

II. Cold Crow Weather

Under the Porch

In a drift of sawdust, shadows
and long strands of web,
in the smell of damp,
mineral-laden dirt, that toad

hunched under our porch,
fattened on what black dreams
fell through the cracks.

Daily we walked up the three steps,
over the creaking board and into the house
knowing it was down there,
forgetting it was down there.

Into the soup went the hambone.
Mother stirred while little brother in his corner
cried, his sobs carrying over

the tv's cantata of bad news, canned laughter.
Outside, the leaves turned red.
My older brother crouched near me
at the edge of the carport roof, considering

our chances. "You jump first," he ordered
and so I did. Khaki-colored grass
rose up to greet me and my brother

followed—what choice did he have?
After a hard rain toad squatted
on the walk, his gnarly skin
like cold sand speckled with gravel.

Evenings, his low croak
traveled up through the floorboards
and into the soles of my feet

as my mother watched the window
turn into a dark mirror,
and my father scraped a match, lit
another Camel. Coughed.

Sweet Molasses

In a basement room the music teacher's hands
lift and fall, white birds on the keyboard.

Smelling of cinnamon, Danny Morgan leans toward me,
humming his two flat notes. Lorraine Rothman

opens her large pink mouth to sing like a bell,
her tongue a clapper refusing to rest. Every song

a river and we, the fifth graders, living stones
the music burbles over and past. I watch

the teacher's hands turn into white canoes.
My brother with the patience of a rock

untangles my fishing line. We sway together
in the wooden boat as mist lifts slowly from the lake.

"Well sweet molasses, you are a peck of trouble
to take along," he tells me, like a grandfather.

Because it was Papa who taught us how to fish.
My brother loosens another knot, hands me

the last piece of melon and a knife to cut it with.
New moon dipped into well-water, it tastes that cool,

that smooth. And so I fall into the green grass
of my brother's kindness. November, though, is nothing

but a cage of dead leaves and drafty school rooms.
I take off my shoe and watch it sail toward the window.

Kiddo is sent home with a note for Mother to read.
For the rest of her life that girl hates saddle shoes

and basements. Lorraine draws boxes of words, steps neatly
across them into a judge's robes, ticking all the while

like a clock. Danny Morgan disappears, so that every
year or two, in a crowd, I spy the back of his curly head.

Silence and Disorder

Start a ruckus. Share that interior sizzle
and you'll be banished. To be quiet, well-behaved—

that's the first lesson. Still, something in me
kept refusing to lie down. I wanted to yodel

or hang by the knees, a pendulum. Energy made me—
and how do you kill that? Sit still, don't shout.

But I could do six backward somersaults
before running out of room. At night sometimes

I listened to stars calling out with their voices of silver light.
In school I'd stare out the window, feeling the chaos

of the universe zinging around. Wind in the branches
and loops of blue radiance stretched tight

and quivering, rubber bands of light. I tried to find
the wormhole. Sometimes in empty fields

or late at night, I could feel my way through.
Cave of silence, inner sight.

I threw stones at a neighbor's house. An engine
drove me to it. To get as close I could to breaking

a window without quite hitting it. I cried
when the window broke. Aria of stone hitting the almost

window—gone now for good. Leaving just me. Bad
and unstill. Summers I'd perch in a rusty tree till lunch.

Beetles bore into the bark, buzzed off. Isinglass
wings carrying their solid bodies away.

Later I'd spin like a top. Fall down, the world
still spinning. Which was truth finding me.

Optical Longings and Illusions

after Man Ray

"Kinetic energy, write this down," Mr. Lewis said.
Chemical reactions. Zigzagging
through the corridors, I colored myself in.

The blackboard marked with chains
of letters, pluses and minuses clustering
around them. Circles, arrows. Longing

as loss of electrons. I saw constellations
missing their lucky stars, random lines
connecting emptiness to emptiness

across the dark night that had us surrounded.
Oh Mr. Lewis. Big ears and bow ties.
But there was something he knew—

dark matter. Chalk dust to me. My elemental
landscape was tending toward train tracks,
bridges suspended over air. Snow, melting.

"Gravitational laws," he said. Changing forms.
Desk to desk, we passed back the mimeographs
with their purple ink. Inhaled their fumes

as if life alone was not enough to make us dizzy.
My best friend turned into a paper doll.
I watched her disappear. Solar flare.

Cold Crow Weather

The meadow is buried in cold negation
and a bully-bright sun wants to knock

you over. Squinting, half-blind, you watch
a spill of crows flap past the frozen field

where you hesitate. Breathing out.
Their heavy black bodies, their purple shine,

their raucous lack of care. You've trekked
in your cousin's army jacket past

the hard rippled stream, ragged hems
of your jeans choked with ice.

You swipe at your nose with a stiff
powdered glove. Under the pines, the snow

is bluish, but out here it glitters like all the lies
you've half-believed. You used to know

how to feel. You want to smash something,
you need to break through everything

that refuses to happen. If only your bony
shoulders could grow black wings.

You tramp and tramp, away
from equations that leave you unnerved.

A chunk of broken brick in your pocket is easier
to handle. You hurl it hard at the frozen stream,

but after a crack and a sharp little leap,
the brick just skitters off, spinning toward snow.

Locked In

When the still blue air gave itself over
to clamoring, I allowed it to take me too,
my eyes on the vee-shaped flock,
thinking it was late for them to be leaving,
the year's cold had come so hard and early.

Lavender sunset and then the winter night,
smell of wood smoke, tiny eyes
blinking in the distance, sharp and bright.
Three times I woke up as trees cracked
and snapped, the chill breaking them.

Next morning, hunched into a walk
with the dog, a quick and muffled lean
into unfriendly air, I spied it— forlorn
hummock of a single goose at rest
on the frozen pond. No. Locked in.

A coyote could have stepped across
that silver surface, made quick work of it.
A snapper could have feasted
on the bird's soft underside.
It craned its neck, let out a soft bleat.

My dog started, barked one sharp reply,
and tugged me home. Later, as the sky
darkened, I checked the pond again.
A trail of patches, the thistle-dark of water
refrozen, led across the pond, shards of ice

scattered in heaps near each spot. And there
near a bush the goose glared toward me,
its battered beak pointed into the wind. The dog
lunged toward it, and the goose blundered
a little away, flapped, resettled.

After long hammering at ice
it made a hole to drag itself into,
and again the same, till hole by hole, it reached
that bit of moving water near the shore
and was free. But too exhausted to fly.

Next day we crunched through again,
the sun a pale lozenge on a pewter plate.
No feathers on the ground, no blood—
I checked. Air in my nostrils cold
enough to sting, we moved on.

And though I never saw it, I'd swear
I heard the sound of beating wings.

Playing House

He played a man going to work,
which felt strange to him, so that he had
to clear his throat loudly three times
every day before walking out the door.

I played Let's Make a Baby.
Something in me kept longing
for the scent of fresh-mown grass
drifting through the window on a summer morn.

That kind of fortune—something I might
fall into if I arranged myself just right. He himself
couldn't go near the mower, of course.
Allergic. What he longed for

was something he'd seen on a billboard,
on TV, on a beer commercial. It spoke
to the chemicals that fizzed around
in his body. Made his hair grow faster.

The day the sky turned green and hail
banged all around him as the car started
its slow slide off the road, my pale
husband told me he'd never bargained

for any of this. I wanted to hold him.
Wanted to deny any guilt. I wanted him to be
the man he could not be. We were
small people trying to make a grown-up life,

something to withstand the elements.
But sometimes marriage tasted
like orange rayon bowling shirts. I wished
I could jump in a wooden boat and row and row

toward an island I'd seen in a dream. Sometimes
he took his brother to the theme park. Rode
the rollercoaster a dozen times. He looked
like a firecracker that had fizzled

when finally he came home. We knew each other
about as well as people bumping carts in the market,
comparing cans of soup. A fistful of coupons
instead of romance. Still, we had our boy, our girl.

But he kept losing parts of himself
in a flurry of jobs that dissolved
like ice in the bottom of a drink. His eyes
began to resemble rocks. I planted tomatoes,

hung laundry out to dry, listened carefully
to crickets, wondering what they could tell us
of the future. Then there was that night
a flaming chunk of rock hurtled through

a neighbor's roof. We moved away.
Ancient stone cottage owned by the mice
in the walls—that's what took us in.
The kitchen held not a single cabinet,

only a chipped enamel table with a drawer
for spoons. It was always winter there,
always snowing. A puff of gray feathers died
on the windowsill, and the baby kept getting

the croup. Up with the child at midnight,
I looked out to see the full moon
had the clouds lit up—they looked
like pillow cases flown off the line.

And there were the crooked prints
my boots had made days before, when they
took off without me, coming home
long after dark, looking lacerated.
Slowly I began to grow up.

Taste of Winter

for every dollar we didn't have
another inch of snow

that year there was so much
we did not have

and so much snow

shifting in the shadow branches
that fell across the yard

it dreamed in silence
and for the first time my own dreams
remained invisible and blank

far away, cars carried people into their lives

my children in their too-small coats
scooped fresh snow into blue bowls

into each bowl I poured
a rich stripe of maple syrup

snow ice cream

they licked the bowls clean

the last crystal
melting on my daughter's lip
looked like a light going out

for every dollar we didn't have
an invention, a new game, a memory

laid down, cold but sweet

as good, I hoped, as money in the bank

Mother in the Month of May / II

Three years after my father's death,
two years after my husband turned
ex, one month after my mother relented,
at last, so that delicate instruments
could skim across her clouded eyes,
remove the damage—
she and I go walking.

It's the first week in May
and we carry nothing with us
as we enter long grass that's not just green,
but sun-bright with dandelions and purple
with violets, heal-all, indigo brush.

Storms have left two trees
stretched out along the ground
and an old dogwood's leaning,
its trunk divided, half jagged,
riddled with woodpecker holes.
The other half is stoutly branching,
thick with a chorus of leaves—
among them small white moons,
the glow of blossoms.

It's the first week in May,
and my mother, grown smaller,
walks now without stumbling, without
holding on. "Look at all the colors;
I've never seen such colors." She lifts
her chin and squints out through sunlight
at the unpeopled field, her eyes unveiled.

A Book, a Bird, a Question

Love, your eyes change daily, blue to green
and back, like a pebble I once held, entirely made of sea.

What's constant— our foolishness, its warp and weft,
its dailiness. If you'd weave from it a blanket,

it would become my only comfort. Instead
you leave your book of numbers open near my chair

and whistle yourself away. A traveler lifts his hand
to knock. Home, he says, is what you must leave

in order to feel its currents, its unrelenting draw.
And then he sighs, drops his scuffed leather case.

The valise opens and a bird rides out on the wind
through a door that bangs open again and again.

The curve of its flight unfurls like sail or memory,
circles back and hangs in the air for one

long moment as it wonders at fire in the window.
Everything leaves us, even the sun. Dusk

is an animal with dark, moist eyes. It comes this close,
but is never quite tamed. The whiteness of a single tree,

unreeling its bark at twilight, is it a reflection? You shrug.
It hardly matters. The number of atoms in the universe

does not alter. But I want to know, if you look for me
a thousand years from now, where will I be?

Mother in the Month of May / III

The twilight darkens. Pond water laps at the grass. Unreadable, its depths, but three stones begin to rise from them, mossy and sleek, perfectly dome-shaped. Sea turtles from worlds I can't imagine. Stepping stones—I am meant to cross over them. How deep is this backyard pond, how ancient, how strange? That small string of lights far off beyond water, is it someone's party? Faint sounds: ice cubes clinking in a glass? I can feel my foot slipping, beginning the long slide into murky waters. No! Wake me up. I call my teen-aged son to the window, wanting him to share this strangeness; he refuses. If he leaves his room, the whole house will be empty, each door opening only to shadow, gray space, stale air. My mother won't return; my son shuts his door. Only these moonlit domes call out to me with their silence. Stepping stones. But they've come from a mystery too deep, too full of shadows. I say no to my mother's leaving. No, I will not follow. Not even my eyelids can move now. Tired is an old song, repeating, repeating. The sea turtles wait. I'm trying to understand this odor of brown leaves littering the edges of the pond. Smoky sweetness of the slow dissolve. From its invisible perch, a nightbird cries. Small, unreachable stars—their lights in the distance glitter.

Untethered

On horseback she waded
into this very river. Right there
she lost the last button
of her blue jacket. Her scarf
loosened too, sailed away,
became a streak of cloud.

Kid catching crayfish thought he saw
some of her regrets, snagged
on the stems of water weeds.

You know how sky and water
darken, reach toward each other,
touch? They say that's when
she lost herself, just as the light
was leaving. Thirty miles
down river her horse turned up,
showing the whites of its eyes.

What Comes to Us

The one we thought we wanted
is not the one we needed.

The one we thought we had
is not the one we got.

For most of a lifetime
we move along dreaming.

In the mirror an exile
stares out, completely baffled.

Finding ourselves in darkness;
at last we can see.

The stray dog on our doorstep
traveled miles to reach us.

Traveled miles to reach us;
it's on the doorstep now.

A Field in August

In the last fine days of August
we find the field of Queen Anne's Lace,
a confusion of snowflakes nodding
on their woody stems to the music
of cicadas.

The dog buries his nose in tall grasses,
chuffing in a world of scents beyond
my ken while I take the sunlight
into my skin, and the cool breeze
that's just now skimmed toward us
from the lake.

This is the dog that came to us
on the eve of a blizzard, skinny
and scarred, shivering hard—
yelping on our doorstep.

This is the field that months ago
was weighted with snow, drifts
that wouldn't let go. The flowers
teetering up toward summer's clear
dry light seem to remember

something of that. You'll say this
can't be true: a thatch of flowering
weed has no capacity for imagination.
The dog leans into my leg, looking
up at me. A fly lands on his back
and he shivers it off.

I say each season, each body, each
living field holds some memory
of days past, some whiff of days to come.

Goodbye, Goodbye

I'll miss you like a blue piano.
I'll miss you the way a healing wound misses its stitches.
I'll miss you like a letter sent to the wrong address.
I won't miss the deep water of your silences
but I'll miss the way your hair
floats away from your head like a cloud.
I'll miss you as the white fox misses the snow
evaporating into mist.
I'll miss you hunched behind the wheel
not caring where you're going.
I won't miss the shadows under your eyes
that remind me of difficulties
because I never want to admit difficulties.
I'll miss you like the message in a bottle
lost in a clog of weeds.
I'll miss you the way a pool hall misses midnight.
I'll miss your lips floating off to sea.

Still Life with Goldfish

After she called, sobbing,
and came home, the skin
near her eyes looking bruised

after he threatened, pleaded, swore
his life would be ashes,
that only she could save him

she returned to him
and the world could not find its way
into my blind eyes.

Only the glass bowl
left on her dresser, the glazed castle
within it, a fish speckled black

barely finning as it hovered there,
only that drew me
and the golden one circling

round and round the other fish,
the helpless flag of its ragged tail.

Wolf Tracks

after Sandy Parisky

We may lose the early jonquils, covered now
in snow, and my daughter's rushing off again,
in her car that keeps falling apart. My work's impossible.
I leave it, trudge the river trail—a little wild,

a little lonely; the wind lives there. I've seen a wolf
near a bend in the river, skinny and gray, and today
in the half-frozen mud, near clumps of saw grass
edged with ice, I find its tracks. I think about hunger.

The way we trot forward into the wind
trying to outrun it. I'm hurrying too
my coat collar up, as the river trail darkens
and the pines gloom into each other, thick as smoke.

Slabs of bedrock, cold and gray, slope toward the river.
Its archipelago of ice floes, its restless churn.
Everything rushing toward change, the colors
melting into each other: midnight blue and silver, hints of violet.

This morning my hairbrush held three silver hairs.
And day after day, my daughter falls into the arms of a man
who won't even meet my eyes. Above the ice-clogged
river, a pair of crows hector a hawk. I move into the space

between their wings. Return to earth. Within the hollow
of each paw print are small caves of shadow.
The day turns to night, river ice breaks away,
turns to water, and all of it runs toward the sea.

A Sea of Stingrays

I'm perfectly calm, I told him. Perfectly.
Calm. The steam you see

is this iron. Not
that you'd know an iron from a colander.

I'm ironing your fussy pin-striped shirts
and putting too much starch in them

because I am not angry. That scorch
mark's on the tail, the part you need to tuck in

so don't start carping at me.
It'll never show. Like some people

never show although they've promised,
although it's important.

I left then—a residue dry as paste
on my tongue. And now I've exiled myself

to this place where the ground
is hard and frozen, where ice begins

to creep over dark waters. The look on his face.
Clouds sliding across the pond

silvery still and flat. But here
is a clutch of yellow leaves, disrupting everything,

a castoff skin huddling on water's shallow edge.
My eyes fall into them and they carry me

to where water once turned strangely
from blue to gold beneath our boat.

That startling gleam: a sea of golden rays
migrating, thousands of them. Seeing them, I lost track

of every thought that held me up. Named them
battalion-of-jets, sky-full-of-kites,

breeze-herding-leaves-all-turned-the-same-way.
Gliding together, a wave without end.

Yet how singular each domed head. And the smooth
skin slightly different on each one: olive,

drab, umber, bronze or gold. One was coffee brown.
My god how like ghosts, almost entirely silent

and carrying their long stingers behind, spears
of poison for anyone who might blunder near them.

Her Turn in the Desert

Mud and straw—the walls
of her new home. Humble like the earth.
She rubs her hand along a wall, feeling
the idea of ancestors, though her own
lived green lives among trees.

Wind and sky,
that's what she needs,
dry heat soaking into the skin,
the light so harsh
it can sear the logic right out.

To be scorched clean
of all that has cluttered her life, to find
the burning center—these are her reasons
for coming here. The desert is rock
and shattered rock. It suits her.

Because her heart clamors so
she needs emptiness,
the balm of it.
She walks east at sundown and sees
sometimes a purple band

rising from the horizon, separating
from all that is rooted,
vanishing from view.
Is that how love goes, a great wing
that rises away and dissolves

into sky, leaving
and returning, leaving again?
She walks
and the earth turns until its shadow,
a great dark halo, flies off.

On the Day of Her Death

she bent to hug us both,
then straightened her spine,
packed us off. Past buttes
and canyons we drove, the sky
unreeling before us, so large, so close,
we could feel its blue energy.

We almost missed
the petroglyphs, duck-heads
and spirals, horned animals, shapes
like small human hands.
Messages
we could not decipher.

Cliffs rose up in their hard baked
skins, ochre in all that sunlight.
Beware of Falling Rocks—
but we felt no danger. Summer.
Our lives seemed perfect, the two of us
together, far from routine.

I remember the scent of sage
sharp in the air, and a hawk
hanging motionless, the only shadow.
How could we have known
what she refused to tell us?
Her small signals unreadable.

We couldn't begin to imagine
the way her secret sadness, her resolve
would rise up like the cliffs—
tall, austere, changing the landscape
of our lives. We drove on into the desert,
its immense emptiness.

The Path through Mystery Is Never a Straight Line

Crimson, purple and black,
spiral, slash and dot—a polyglot
of colors and forms bear down
on me from paintings she abandoned

here with us. I move
as though underwater, currents
I can't name pushing against me,
sifting through me.

My breath is a small creature
creeping from its shell. I must
turn to the music of her art,
try to listen. From a field of green,

fern green, jungle green, sudden bursts
of orange race toward the margin,
and a few thin lines spin unsteady,
like laughter, around the edges of it all.

I try to find my way in, as she
must have, her entire life.
She'd say, "The path through mystery
is never a straight line."

At times she found her way.
The answer flicked its tongue at her,
quick as an emerald lizard, before
it disappeared.

For years hieroglyphics
fell into her art, strange symbols
in a language even she could not explain.
I remember her stepping back,

then leaning close toward a canvas
still wet, peering at color, form and line,
aiming toward a translation
that could speak to the human heart.

Legacy of Light and Shadow

The rooms of her house stand silent,
guarding their stillness. But the great tin belly
of the rental truck's been filled, two hundred

canvases wrapped and stacked. The map
with its careful markings lies folded
between us. Having nothing else,
we put our faith in it. We grind down hill,
two thousand miles still to go and hovering

behind us, that cargo of painted dreams.
History of the world as she saw it: feathery grasses,
falling rocks, slashes of golden rain. Beaded pots

that shimmered with hues of light
on calm waters. The lean of a lotus.
In the wound of her sudden absence,
I wonder how to stretch my arms wide enough
to take in all she's left us.

The roof of our truck, a thin metal sheet,
rattles and bangs like thunder. Words
fade away. We pass red rocks, yellow grass,

black cattle scattered in fields. No trees.
Shadow floating across dry pasture, then
a hawk swooping down toward something
we can't see. That shadow, if we could see it
hanging silent above us, ready to change everything,

would we manage differently? For a while
the truck shimmies and shakes, then settles down.
A steady groan, eating up the miles.

Evening wanders down from the mountains.
Into the softening light my husband squints,
his neck jutting forward. There is a kindness
between us, a sense that what we have
is fragile, rare. We should take care.

Wheat Field with Crows

after Vincent van Gogh

From fields lush with wheat
they rise up, those old black
sorrows, crying out my name,
taking pleasure in it too. Like the stiff
straw men abandoned there,
coming unhinged, they flap
and stir the chaff to storms
of golden dust. What crooked rut
is this that wanders, a little green,
into the grain toward
the squawking of crows?
Even when I believe I've left
the world's restless errands behind,
an agitation follows me.
In this incandescent world
the sky comes roiling closer,
bearing again its difficult night.

Trying to Teach Travis

On his arm he's drawing two snakes;
his fingers are busy and green.
His beautiful eyes are great salt lakes
and his mind is a submarine.

His fingers are busy and green
and I ask for his homework in vain.
This boy's mind is a submarine
and his book was left out in the rain.

I ask for his homework in vain.
His sister ran off last night
and his book was left out in the rain.
He says there was some kind of fight.

His sister ran off last night.
He's pouring a puddle of glue.
He says there was some kind of fight
but the things that were shouted aren't true.

He's pouring a puddle of glue.
His beautiful eyes are great salt lakes
and the things that were shouted aren't true.
On his arm he's drawing two snakes.

Thirteen Ways of Looking at a Classroom

after Wallace Stevens

I

Early morning, before the students arrive,
a single movement flickers in the hallway—
bulb on the fritz.

II

The loudspeaker announces
a moment of silence.
Among 24 students there is never
silence.

III

Sometimes when I'm teaching
the schoolgirl I used to be
returns. Each self pauses
for a moment,
wondering what the other one is doing.

IV

The teacher and her students
make a round number.
The substitute circles and circles,
looking for a way in.

V

Six hands, waving in the air—
their enthusiasm beautiful.
Tentative knowledge
lighting a shy child's face
has its own beauty.

VI
In the rectangular room
in the glow of flat screens
our young click and scroll.
Is it possible
to think outside the box?

VII

From the whiteboard I erase
the day's objective.
At twilight I drive home
past mounds of cindered snow. Tonight
I'll dream of peacocks and green rivers.

VIII

Girls shuffle to their seats
in bedroom slippers. In pile-lined boots.
Boys saunter toward the back row.
Heads shaved. Their ears that do not listen
are adorned with chips of glass and metal.

IX

I know they need to discover
their own voices, the deep truths
of their lives. Yet every day
I exhort them "Please—be quiet!"

X

The boy who loses his papers
has one ear that sticks out
more than the other. The girl
who's allergic to nuts
has exploding hair.

XI

No one will sit in the chair
of the student who died.
I read a poem aloud and pause.
We feel the dead child listening.

XII

A red-tailed hawk lands
on the roof right outside our room.
I am the wind that held it up.
I am the window. And I am the students
hunched over their tests,
blind to the world.

XIII

When the last bus leaves
on the final day of June
a crumpled paper
skitters across the asphalt
after it.

Boys

Arm farts, balls thumping against a scuffed wall,
trample of big feet. Water dripping from the ceiling,
accelerating its riff as the shower above
thrums on, oblivious to high seas—

such is the masculine music
a mother of sons learns to live with.
The garden loses its roses; sweat socks
bloom on the banister.

In the sallow light
of the Frigidaire, a boy's cheekbones glow,
surfaces of a waxing moon.
That noise? Heavy Metal—

my boys' idea of what music should be.
A woman wants to walk beneath trees,
but her sons are sucked into screens
raucous with Pow! Kablam!

Such triumph in their laughter.
I tell my boys "Don't
jump from airplanes." They laugh.
They hurl themselves into the void.

The body still remembers: their rolls, their hiccups,
experimental jabs. I was heavy with them.
Soon it was black belts,
giant sandwiches, helicopters, war.

The things they must have.
I held my first son over the red, red blooms
of tulips and his hands flew toward them
like birds. "Dat! Dat!" he crowed

at each new thing he wanted. Clouds
passed over us, geese, the long tails of comets.
Lost father. Hole in the wall. A guitar
wailing through the night.

We peeled oranges, we bit down,
a fine spray of juice entering the air.
My youngest boy ran back and forth
in the mall, watching his sneakers light up.

Joy! His eyes flashed, joy!
Until his brothers made fun. "I'm not crying,"
he told me. "I never really feel any sadness."
These late winter evenings the furnace

clicks on like a querulous voice.
In the closet's last shadow, a ball deflates.
Back of the vegetable bin something soft
folds in upon itself. The cat curls into a small

spot of sun. No bicycles lean on the lawn,
no skateboards, no wrenches.
Clouds pass over me, geese,
the long tails of comets.

Living Room

for Owen

For now the war is silent,
folded on the coffee table, inky smudge
of smoke, young man's dark eyes
left to stare at the ceiling.
Tomorrow he'll be recycled.
There are many ways to disappear

but we've planted ourselves right here.
We've painted our living room red,
hung mountains on the walls
and trees and clouds,
a few slender boats like the slimmest of moons
rocking on gray water.

Tenderness and Slaughter
I've named my two hands. Sometimes
I enter the meadow and follow it
into birches suspended above the couch.
The yellow leaves stir
and feathery grasses brush at my skin.

Another mission: my son straps in.
He flies in darkness—
harder to track him that way.
There are good ways to disappear
but my heart is a desert. He moves
through a heat rising up, a rug
he must breathe through.

And I can't subdue
the room inside me, the way it murmurs
like a stony stream, what if, what if…
When I switch off the lamp, its filaments
crack and pop.

Night's river of pictures will not stop.
I hold a white cloth and gently wash
an infant's face. I'm picking up stones,
weighing their heft, their talent for damage.
For hours I look for lost luggage, trudging
through a city of bells, ringing and ringing,
gold domes, and rubble in the streets.

Within me's a room of red heat
and things that float like bats, all shadow.
We don't talk about fear
but we've painted our living room red.
The mantle's bone white
and the clouds rushing over that lake,
they're splitting open; I watch them break.

Kandahar

after Virginia Dehn

Single handprint on the wall
where so much has been erased.
In the breath of a whisper
a candle flickers.
The carpet's intricate patterns
a language beyond words, a history,
a genotype, generation of dreams,
one laid over the other, over the other.
O Kandahar, the woman who painted you
is gone, the man in the whitewashed house
is gone. My lanky son in goggles
that make him strange, a helmet
clamped over his thinning red hair,
why is he there—
in the whirlwind of your refusal?
The cloth on the wall is frayed.
Behind it a fretwork of messages.
Red dots, blue boxes, cuneiform.
What is history, Kandahar?
What is love? When will we remember
what it is to be human? In this
charged world of our own making,
how will we grow the right kind of skin?

Zen Garden

Five dark rocks,
gray gravel raked
into circles around them.

I, who love the world,
retreat from it here.

High overhead,
light and darkness,
branches of old trees sway.

Birdsong
spills into this silence.

What can prayer be
but a small, still space
close to the city's center?

Five dark rocks, the moon rising.

III. Blue Door

Evolution as Longing and Escape

It began with steam rising up
through grates on the sidewalks.
The city stretching itself, not just
into a gritty sky, but down below

tunneling into a history obscured
by concrete. What I walked on
was nothing solid after all, but a kind
of bridge between two things

I could not see the ends of. This was
before I had children, although they came to me
in dreams. What was childhood anyway,
but a Band-aid I'd just pulled off?

And underneath—this pale thin self
that might dissolve. Some days I'd walk
the 20 blocks to work, watching
men rattle the cages off shop entrances.

The need for people to want things.
The need for metal bars.
We evolve unevenly toward restraint,
finally losing ourselves.

Once I dodged a little girl, her head full
of braids, as she walked backward, chanting.
Most days I meandered
through my brother's Erector set constructions,

flimsy pipe and plywood scaffolds
laid against a patchwork of buildings.
Rainy days I'd join the shadow figures, people
whose lives barely nudged against my own,

peering down a tunnel, waiting for whatever rush
of metal and noise would come for us, take us away.
Where was the stop that would lead me
to a grown up life? End of the line

I imagined, longing would dissipate.
Clerks in the bookstore
where I worked were all somebody else—
actress, musician, playwright.

Michael ate soup for a year, patching
together funds for his next trip, to Mongolia
where he'd herd yaks with the natives.
He did it, too. But me? Third floor walk-up

with its narrow cot, cracked door
scavenged from the street
to make a countertop, desk, a table.
Stockings flung over the shower curtain—

shadows of someone climbing toward escape.
On Saturday night another lost boy
leaning toward me in the Italian restaurant,
hoping to be rescued.

Ambition

first ascent above the Arctic Circle in a hot air balloon:
Edward Daniel Clarke, 1799, in Swedish Lappland

***

Arctic Circle, glittering bracelet of ice.
The Midnight Sun—its round, pale light.
And there on the ground, white globe of satin paper, edged in red.
Cotton ball soaked in alcohol, set aflame,
its ruby glow breathing life into the fabric.

***

What was flat begins to sit up.
Inflated hopes.

***

Laplanders arrive, converge around the balloon as it bulks out.
Step backward then, into their own shadows.
A wariness.
Footprints in traces of snow.

***

The most timid among the human race, Clarke calls them.

***

And he a man who spends his life
trying to escape from himself
puts his explorations on a leather thong,
wears them like magic charms, an amulet.

***

Reindeer mill about, tear at shrubs with their practical yellow teeth.

***

The balloon rises at last into clear evening air.
Much shouting and hallooing.
But rolling their eyes and huffing their breath
the reindeer scatter.
The Lapps run after them.

***

There are designs on paper and then
the chaos of real life.

***

Clarke's balloon tilts, slides, struggles for altitude
skims a lake.
Rises again, phantom-like, dripping and uncertain.
Sails a good quarter mile,
crashes.

***

Do we dream our lives into being?
Clarke continues undaunted,
brave, foolish, in love
with the sun and the moon.

***

And what silken moon was that
fell past the green flickering flames
of the aurora borealis
into their world for a while?
The Laplanders wonder

***
even as they imagine
they can attach themselves
to the long, untranslatable, silver stream
of reindeer
moving through the tundra like stars through time.

Periscope

Her voice like bees, it's never
        left him. Her mouth a hummingbird.

Shimmer, then flit out the window
        where he'll follow. Today's shimmer—

driveway slick with ice. Air breaking open
        to an anxious spinning of wheels.

Lack of traction. The world losing itself
        in snowy drifts. He disappears

into memory: white deer lifting its head
        from the tall ferns of a wild place.

Its long neck rising up like a periscope—
        middle of an emerald sea.

Periscope, his memory swivels
        toward that day. Was it a ghost

he'd been staring at? Another
        version of himself, startled

by the world, separate
        from the place others seem to inhabit?

Today's wind the voice of an absence
        he'll paint on the walls of his chapel.

His thoughts are green islands,
    floating from sea to sea.

You could say he's not getting anywhere,
    he's lost in a wild place with hummingbirds

and bees. Above, the shimmer of a silver plane,
    unearthly, hanging there.

The False Mirror

after René Magritte

Sheep on the hill, whitecaps in the sea, clouds drifting through a blue that is generous and wide—and a flat black disc in the midst of it, dark side of the sun. Light is nothing without darkness. Does this happen to you? Do you fall into the things you see, do they begin to fill you? The sheen of gasoline swirling on a puddle's surface, old woman's ragged sweater limping into view—when you see these things, do you get a physical feeling? We learn to think with symbols, dream a symbolic landscape. Seeing one thing, we understand, it's really something else. But where is truth without the curves of the solid? Say two pears lean toward each other on the wooden table. Their skins are mottled golden, brown and blush, their curves held together by shadows. The sky would be an emptiness without the shifting forms of clouds. Standing in their shadows, I feel the drift of darkness, how it flows through the light of our world. I want to know all the ways we are blind. I want to open my large terracotta eye. I want to stare and stare and stare.

Double Vision

    you don't always recognize rain   that liquid we move through
        it puffs itself into clouds—   sleeps in laundry on the line

          the idea of it hovers   over the garden

          sometimes I'm matter   sometimes anti-matter
my twin and I near identical   but split; we can't combine

        the unnoticed world teems   with palindromes
           write a word, a phrase   left to right to left

dogesseseegod   do geese see god

    we're rolling along in a wave of time   we're always
all ways, forward and back, sideways   existing in so many planes

        at once, light refracted   through a raindrop

myself and I move along   together, in opposite directions
    through a rain-splashed street   I love the way our feet touch

    the earth, the wet ground   sneakers saying splat, squelch, splat
          sticking a little   wanting to linger

stepping through and over puddles—   mirrors that quiver and flatten
   they shimmer unnoticed beneath our feet   shining illusions of stillness

    casually, we step over trees   leaves lacy beneath our knees
        rooftops balancing   on their triangular points

      puddles are dreams of sky   sky is a languid lake
          where geese paddle   toward no deity I can name

         my twin and I   try to write ourselves into existence
          InwordsdrownI   In words drown I

As We Were Leaving the National Zoo

my young son planted his feet
in front of the cage.
Hunched inside—a huge, hairy
football player, sidelined, morose.
No. A philosopher,
brow furrowed, small eyes dark.
Long, long thoughts. What we saw
was nothing natural.
Ape-in-a-Box.

I don't know
what possessed my skinny son to scrunch
up his face and stick out his tongue that way.
Even the prisoner scratched his furry chin
before making
exactly the same face back.

My kid jumped up
as if a small firecracker
had gone off inside his belly.
Sunburned knees and a short ha ha.
Then he stood still, concentrating,
and vibrated his thin lips.
A rude noise. Waggled his fingers.
Magic! The same thing back.
There was Mr. Inscrutable spitting out
Blaatt!
and the dark palms opening, closing,
digits moving in sign language
or as if some little birds
had flown into the cage in error.

Dusk settled in. Our feet cried out to us
and the clouds looked tattered. It was time
to go. But no, no, no—
I don't remember
my son's exact questions,
just that he had so many of them.
Tug on the hand, another question.
Tug on the hand, the voice rising.

Tug, the high color in his cheeks,
his hair damp at the temples, around the ears
and his eyes feverish, shiny.
As we pulled him away, my child
kept twisting around, turning his head,
looking back.

Because of the Oranges

In the back of the car, a dozen oranges
roll out of the sack, thump around till I pull over.
Fix it, stand there for a minute in the late slant
of sun, watching yellow leaves swirl into
small tornadoes and flurry away.
A single car whooshes past and then

they amble out of the woods, four wild turkeys,
pecking at weeds, lifting the curves of their necks up
for a burst of gabble and cluck. Now they turn
into a motorcycle gang, a muscled swagger
of misfits that begins to surround me.
And the wind picks up, dust lifting up

from the roadside, stinging a little. I just stand there,
holding my palms up. I'm innocent, unarmed.
They burst into furious gabbles, making
their judgments, their heads nodding and one
stretches out its wings, flies low across
the deserted road, right past me, so I hear

the riffle of air as the huge wings brush by.
For a moment it feels like the shadow of death.
It feels like something holy. I have become
an island in the middle of a great stillness,
even as three wild birds come almost to my feet,
bobbing their heads and daring, just daring

me to do something about it. The neck and head
of the largest is very red, almost obscene,

but the pattern of its feathers could be polished wood,
smooth russet and gray, and a very deep brown.
I want to reach out and touch it. I want to get
the heck out of there. All this takes place in a minute—

maybe two, that elongates, rubber band-like,
until the redhead makes as if to peck at me.
The others jabber like maniacs and I reach behind me
to the car door and get in. Even then they continue
to surround me—a visitation I'm still, 30 miles away
and a day later, trying to fathom.

Lunar Eclipse

Can you hear the sky, how it streams
the notes of an aria lost long ago? It's the moon
dreaming again. Or we ourselves are lost
in some dream, beneath a trail of cloud

as the moon edges into earth's shadow, begins
to glow like a pomegranate. You told me once
my heart was cold as a marble. You couldn't see
how it ached like this moon pulsing red, beyond

the touch of anyone, out there in its universe
of silence. Lens of a camera, pupil of an eye
open wider and wider, never knowing why
certain bodies, moving into their inevitable

positions, bawl out their brief transformation.
O dress me in a golden sari, kimono of red silk
patterned with birds that wing across
a bronze-colored sea—do that if you would know

a different sort of me. That cold planet
spinning into and through the penumbra
is pitted with ancient accidents. You touch
your shoulder to mine and streaks of cloud

begin to loosen, move away. Out there
The Sea of Tranquility croons to its dust. We lean into
the night's strangeness. The round syllables
of an owl's call fall toward us and we swallow them.

Illusion as Snake in the Grass

This alien thing, so silent
and legless. But beautiful too—
whisper of green, a sigh parting
and reforming the field grass.
Is it illusion, this grace
when the grass gently sways
in the shine of the day, water
stirred by a paddle? Swift
undulations moving sideways
and ahead at the same time—
doesn't that sudden glimpse
brush against an ordinary day
like the eyelash of a god?
And it stays somehow—
as a quickening of the breath,
a tingle in the spine,
spine we must bear upright
in our heavy, human, heedless way.

Manatee

Across a rubber raft
I lean my awkward elbows,
watching light on the water break apart
and mend itself, over and over—

until I notice your voluptuous drift.
A blimp trundling lazy and smooth
through water, you're slow

as the nothing days, the nowhere days
that drop away, that turn and turn
into puddles half-remembered.

Your shadow glides, a cloud,
and then you surface, breathing noisily
and I am graced with a glimpse of you,

Buddha of the coastal waters.
Close up I see the rough braid
of scars on your hide—motorboats, propellers.

Whiskered and thick, you are
no mermaid. A solid aunt, perhaps,
comfortable in your body.

Spooling slowly along with your calf,
your mossy back attracting
small darting fish.

Your kind has been on this planet
45 million years. But my kind!
We're careless and greedy.

We damage things.
Still, you ridiculous creature,
with nothing but tenderness in your eyes,
you keep on gliding toward me.

In Flight

One dragonfly is diving into the other
with the tip of its turquoise body
and all the while they're darting around
in the stippled light that bounces over water
as the sun pours down and sparks flash
from the dragonflies' nearly invisible wings.

All across the lake this is happening
and now I understand how light
and delight are coupled too.
They don't have much time, these insects
but they are so wildly alive
that as I watch them I feel dizzy

in love with the dragonflies, with the possibilities
that whiz around us on an ordinary day.
But a little sadness creeps in too,
a little sorrow that my own body
is so well-acquainted with gravity.
I'm wishing I could make love

while flying over the breeze-ruffled water
but this is not going to happen.
Well, joy and regret, they too
stick together, they too catch us up
like the flashing mirrors that are dragonflies
mating midair, over a shimmer of water.

The Unparalleled Beauty of a Crooked Line

after Pat Rosoff's "Pitta Patta"

everything strays
    think of your heart
dragging its load of vagrant arrows

    the city map
        refusing to fold itself flat
    here are the broken lines of avenues

rendered clearly   but where
    are the fire escapes
where are the people who have left us

    like rivers they meander
        through the red clay earth
    and we're meant to follow them

wearing silt   wearing stone
    we float like leaves
in the current   now spinning in place

    now slipping under
        the old stone bridge
    we find the pattern   we come

so close but someone keeps falling
    out of line   making a crooked path
we live   we love   we can't be contained

Balloon Man

The sky is a blue door
and he has opened it.
After years of patching flats,
tightening bolts, breathing in the exhaust
of others as they peeled away, now

he grins in his lawn chair
as 200 balloons lift him up
to sail over a coffee cart,
beyond the light poles. The noise
of a white dog fades away, yap yap
yap, then just the breeze in his hair, soft rush
of motion, a little applause.

And barrels leaning behind the brewery
are a clutter of thimbles, the cars
in the Safeway lot just a pattern of color,
a shiny mosaic. Tower Theatre's tall sign
looks like a tongue depressor held up to the light.

Second attempt: this time
he's done everything right. He's passed
the empty factory surrounded by weeds,
the nursing home where people
stay blanketed in chairs.
Now he floats past fields of sagebrush,
stands of juniper, and now
the high plateau.

His wife loves a tree
called Rose of Sharon. All over the yard
its blossoms fall. He thinks of that as he sees
his shadow glide along our earth,
silent as a flower.

Humming and squeaking in the hands
of the wind, the balloons nudge each other
and it's hard to know if the dream
is this flight
or the life he's fled.

Far below white shirts flap on a line like flags.
They are empty
but he is fat with the green smell of forests
and with all that he's dared. He slugs back some coffee,
pats his pockets for chocolate, the blow darts,
and the BB gun, Red Ryder, to rescue him
should he get too high.

The Snore

Sometimes it's no more
than a loud purring
but it can grumble like a kettle
coming to a boil.
It can be a lawnmower,
the rowdy party next door
you weren't invited to,
marbles rolling across the warped wood
of an old forgotten drawer.
It's thunder in the distance,
storm clouds huffing closer.
Sometimes it's full of enthusiasm,
it gallops and snorts—a horse
refusing to believe it's been tamed.

Most often it's beautifully raucous—
the calls of geese
flying sorrowful and strong
in their crooked formation
as a huge moon rises beyond the trees.
A breeze kicking up, autumn in the air.
The dear imperfection of the living body,
unconscious signature
of the beloved there beside you,
even as he's far away,
beyond speech, journeying
to some place you can never reach.

Ordinary Time

We're on the deck, easy with our drinks,
our faint sunburns, that summer feeling
we've escaped from ordinary time.

They're out at the island, three teenagers
fooling around at the rope swing.
Against the sun we see their silhouettes

swinging back and forth, hear their laughter
and the loud punctuation of young bodies
hitting water. The trick is to swing straight out

and let go at the apex over deep water,
beyond the boulders that lurk
close to shore. One of the boys out at the rope

now swings back and forth, back—
reluctant to face that brief terror
of hanging onto nothing. A girl in the water

laughs at him, shouts, "Michael, come on!"
Wind pushes sheets of silver across the lake,
hiding whatever weeds or stones await

beneath the surface. The boy at last lets go—
there's no way to refuse the future.
His splash joins the others and he surfaces

with a shout that sounds like a yodel.
Closer to us, a child's inflatable ball
floats by, twirling and scudding

as the breeze puffs and pauses.
My thoughts take me to a different lake
and I'm a child again, in a boat

with my brother and Papa. When my grandpa
falls overboard, half the lake rises up,
the rowboat rocks hard and Papa's hat

floats in the long suspense before
he reappears, spouting water like a whale.
He's a beautiful man, huge in his kindness,

exuberant, clumsy. But somehow
childhood dissolves and now Papa
is an old felt hat floating in my memory.

Beside me my husband puts down his beer,
calls the dog to him and for a quick moment
hugs him tight. The dog's white-tipped tail

beats like a metronome. Out at the island
the rope swings empty—the kids head for shore.
Rowdy insults carry over the water.

I turn toward my husband and do not say,
O, what will become of us? And I do not say,
I love sharing these moments with you.

(Oh why, *why* don't I say it?)
Instead I show him the tomatoes,
firm and perfectly ripe. I give him

the fresh fish, ready for grilling.
I slap a mosquito that's stealing
my blood. I chop the basil.

You Reappear

Three days of snow driving hard at the windows,
a sky so heavy it barely holds
itself up. And then this morning arrives—
pristine. The sun a new sun, spectacular

in its sharp cold brilliance—the whole town
bathed in this intense winter light.
And there you are stamping in from the driveway,
peeling off your hat so the white hair

on either side of your head sticks straight out,
electric, and you squint at me as your eyes adjust
to the lesser indoor illumination. You wear
your humanity so plainly, washed and rewashed

in the years we've shared. I confess
that for days I was all but blind to you,
but at this moment I look your way
and maybe it's the angle of sun pouring

through the window—the light you carry
is suddenly visible. It happens like this sometimes,
a shadow slips away and you reappear
fixing the closet door, looking up from your list

of irregular galaxies, or staring into the fire,
sharing your amazement at Beethoven's symphony,
how magnificently it moves us,
and the man himself, you say, your voice hushed

and incredulous, unable to hear it,
though his heart was aflame with music.

Your Heart, Like a Wild Bird, Lands in the Middle of a Life

You are leaving emptiness
behind now. Filling the water jugs,
whispering the long slow
slopes of change, cliff to hill, pale

to purple, evening to dawn. And you on your knees
in a bed of daffodils, the soil offering up
what it's withheld all winter.
Eager the little rabbit in the clover.

Overhead a cloud floating gently.
Silent shadow, the impression of raindrops
in yesterday's dust. Nevertheless, there is kindness.
Small child cradling a blue-feathered bird

with its crooked wing. *I'll hold you.*
The willow a woman, drying her fresh-washed hair.
You remember a handful of berries
from a childhood that is lost

but still sweet. You are so alone.
No you're not.
You are all of us gripping the fence.
Waking up in a quiet room.

Another magnificent morning
at a table with toasted bread.
There's a story that goes…
and now once again it begins.

Red Balloon

after Paul Klee

And I sail into
the unknowable future

a red balloon
that lifts itself

from a place of doors
and windows, no walls

past a freefall of light
into the soft evening air.

I dreamt a tunnel
opening wide, whispering

birth, death, distance
but the mystery

would not reveal itself.
Right now my eyes

are everywhere—at the windows,
in the wind.

Even as I rise past the roof
of my routine, the wish

to linger here is a long
string I dangle.

Great Blue Heron at Elizabeth Park

I stop when I see it standing there,
smoky blue in low waters, a bird
Modigliani might have invented.
Without thinking, I take on its stillness.

My breathing slows, focus sharpens.
Is it telepathy that shapes me,
for a moment, in its image?

And then it leaps into flight, its wings
too large to believe. Unnerving,
its sudden change from slender statue
to menacing motion, to a density

and darkness that makes the pale sky
seem a paltry thing. And though I am
earthbound, clumsy and plain,
something hushed and unsullied stirs.

I feel it, that we can rise above the weight
of our mistakes, that any of us can be,
if only briefly, large against the sky.

Lotus with Seeing Hand

after Virginia Dehn

Hand of its maker in the tapestry,
vision of the weaver

and in this wordless room
so much that's unstill.

Stem of the lotus not quite straight.
White blossom leaning toward the seeing hand.

In the black amphora
sacred oil dreams past its own containment

as near it the white cup opens up
like the mind of a dreamer

or the heart of a bird
early on a morning in May.

On the table a woven cloth of crooked lines
made by the ploughman's wife.

Furrows in deep soil, pale threads lining up
not quite evenly, ribbons in the dark cloth.

Possibilities. The past, the future, the now
in which this blossom continues to grow.

Painting, dream, words that unfurl
on the scroll of the mind,

in the mystery that holds us—
call it time, earthly existence, God—

each label a lie
that is, like art, nonetheless true.

About the Author

Ginny Lowe Connors is the author of *Barbarians in the Kitchen* (Antrim House Books, 2005) as well as a chapbook, *Under the Porch* (Hill-Stead Museum, 2010). She runs a small poetry press, Grayson Books, and is the editor of four poetry collections: *Essential Love, To Love One Another, Proposing on the Brooklyn Bridge,* and *Where Flowers Bloom.* She has won numerous awards for her poetry, including *Atlanta Review's* International Poetry Competition Prize and the 2010 Sunken Garden Poetry Prize. Connors, who holds an MFA from Vermont College of Fine Arts, has been published in many literary magazines and anthologies. An English teacher in West Hartford, Connecticut, in 2003 she was named Poet of the Year by the New England Association of Teachers of English.

This book is set in Garamond Premier Pro, which had its genesis in 1988 when type-designer Robert Slimbach visited the Plantin-Moretus Museum in Antwerp, Belgium, to study its collection of Claude Garamond's metal punches and typefaces. During the mid-fifteen hundreds, Garamond—a Parisian punch-cutter—produced a refined array of book types that combined an unprecedented degree of balance and elegance, for centuries standing as the pinnacle of beauty and practicality in type-founding. Slimbach has created an entirely new interpretation based on Garamond's designs and on comparable italics cut by Robert Granjon, Garamond's contemporary.

To order additional copies of this book
or other Antrim House titles, contact the publisher at

Antrim House
21 Goodrich Rd., Simsbury, CT 06070
860.217.0023, AntrimHouse@comcast.net
or the house website (www.AntrimHouseBooks.com).

•

On the that website
in addition to information on books
you will find sample poems, upcoming events,
and a "seminar room" featuring supplemental biography,
notes, images, poems, reviews, and
writing suggestions.